50 Cakes from Around the World

By: Kelly Johnson

Table of Contents

- Black Forest Cake (Germany)
- Victoria Sponge Cake (United Kingdom)
- Tiramisu (Italy)
- Sacher Torte (Austria)
- Basque Burnt Cheesecake (Spain)
- Tres Leches Cake (Mexico)
- Pavlova (Australia/New Zealand)
- Japanese Cotton Cheesecake (Japan)
- Medovik (Russia)
- Cassata (Italy)
- Chiffon Cake (United States)
- Bolo de Rolo (Brazil)
- Malva Pudding (South Africa)
- Dobos Torte (Hungary)
- Kue Lapis (Indonesia)
- Baumkuchen (Germany)
- Red Velvet Cake (United States)
- Pandan Chiffon Cake (Southeast Asia)
- Mooncake (China)
- Swedish Princess Cake (Sweden)
- Angel Food Cake (United States)
- Mille-Feuille (France)
- Kransekake (Norway)
- Revani (Turkey)
- Lamington (Australia)
- Kladdkaka (Sweden)
- Castella Cake (Japan)
- Fruitcake (United Kingdom)
- Bienenstich (Germany)
- Pastel de Nata (Portugal)
- Esterházy Torte (Hungary)
- Medovnik (Czech Republic)
- Funfetti Cake (United States)
- Hummingbird Cake (Jamaica)
- Rum Cake (Caribbean)

- Coffee Walnut Cake (United Kingdom)
- Zebra Cake (Russia)
- Honey Cake (Armenia)
- King Cake (France/Louisiana)
- Mawa Cake (India)
- Napoleon Cake (Russia)
- Pão de Ló (Portugal)
- Punschkrapfen (Austria)
- Orange Olive Oil Cake (Spain)
- Banana Cake (Philippines)
- Sans Rival (Philippines)
- Buko Pandan Cake (Philippines)
- Chocolate Biscuit Cake (Ireland)
- Dulce de Leche Cake (Argentina)
- Ma Lai Gao (China)

Black Forest Cake (Germany)

Ingredients:

For the Cake:

- 1 ¾ cups all-purpose flour
- ¾ cup unsweetened cocoa powder
- 2 cups granulated sugar
- 1 ½ teaspoons baking powder
- 1 teaspoon baking soda
- ½ teaspoon salt
- 3 eggs
- 1 cup buttermilk
- ½ cup vegetable oil
- 2 teaspoons vanilla extract
- 1 cup hot water

For the Filling and Topping:

- 2 cups heavy whipping cream
- ¼ cup powdered sugar
- 2 cups cherry pie filling
- ¼ cup kirsch (cherry liqueur)
- Chocolate shavings for garnish

Instructions:

1. Preheat oven to 350°F (175°C). Grease and flour two 9-inch round cake pans.
2. In a bowl, whisk together flour, cocoa, sugar, baking powder, baking soda, and salt.
3. Add eggs, buttermilk, oil, and vanilla. Mix until combined. Stir in hot water until smooth.
4. Divide batter into prepared pans and bake for 30–35 minutes. Let cool completely.
5. Brush cake layers with kirsch.
6. Beat heavy cream with powdered sugar until stiff peaks form.
7. Spread cherry pie filling over one cake layer. Top with whipped cream, then place the second cake layer on top.
8. Frost with whipped cream and garnish with cherries and chocolate shavings.

Victoria Sponge Cake (United Kingdom)

Ingredients:

- 1 cup unsalted butter, softened
- 1 cup granulated sugar
- 4 large eggs
- 2 cups self-rising flour
- 2 tablespoons milk
- 1 teaspoon vanilla extract
- ½ cup strawberry jam
- 1 cup whipped cream
- Powdered sugar for dusting

Instructions:

1. Preheat oven to 350°F (175°C). Grease and line two 8-inch cake pans.
2. Cream butter and sugar together until light and fluffy.
3. Beat in eggs one at a time, then fold in flour, milk, and vanilla extract.
4. Divide batter between pans and bake for 20–25 minutes. Let cool.
5. Spread jam and whipped cream on one cake layer, then top with the second layer.
6. Dust with powdered sugar before serving.

Tiramisu (Italy)

Ingredients:

- 6 egg yolks
- ¾ cup granulated sugar
- 1 cup mascarpone cheese
- 1 ½ cups heavy cream
- 2 cups brewed espresso, cooled
- ¼ cup coffee liqueur (optional)
- 24 ladyfinger cookies
- Cocoa powder for dusting

Instructions:

1. Beat egg yolks and sugar until thick and pale.
2. Add mascarpone and mix until smooth.
3. Whip heavy cream until stiff peaks form, then fold into mascarpone mixture.
4. Mix espresso and coffee liqueur in a shallow dish.
5. Dip ladyfingers briefly in espresso and layer in a dish.
6. Spread half of the mascarpone mixture over the ladyfingers. Repeat with another layer.
7. Refrigerate for at least 4 hours, then dust with cocoa powder before serving.

Sacher Torte (Austria)

Ingredients:

For the Cake:

- ½ cup unsalted butter, softened
- 1 cup granulated sugar
- 6 eggs, separated
- 5 oz bittersweet chocolate, melted
- 1 cup all-purpose flour
- ½ teaspoon salt

For the Filling and Glaze:

- ½ cup apricot jam
- 7 oz bittersweet chocolate, melted
- ½ cup heavy cream

Instructions:

1. Preheat oven to 350°F (175°C). Grease and flour a 9-inch round cake pan.
2. Beat butter and sugar until fluffy. Add egg yolks one at a time. Stir in melted chocolate.
3. Fold in flour and salt. In a separate bowl, beat egg whites until stiff peaks form, then fold into batter.
4. Pour batter into pan and bake for 45 minutes. Let cool.
5. Slice cake in half and spread apricot jam between layers.
6. Heat heavy cream, then stir in melted chocolate. Pour over cake. Let set before serving.

Basque Burnt Cheesecake (Spain)

Ingredients:

- 2 cups cream cheese
- 1 cup granulated sugar
- 3 eggs
- 1 cup heavy cream
- 1 teaspoon vanilla extract
- ¼ cup all-purpose flour

Instructions:

1. Preheat oven to 400°F (200°C). Line a springform pan with parchment paper.
2. Beat cream cheese and sugar until smooth.
3. Add eggs one at a time, mixing well. Stir in heavy cream and vanilla.
4. Sift in flour and mix until smooth.
5. Pour batter into pan and bake for 50 minutes until top is deeply browned.
6. Cool before serving.

Tres Leches Cake (Mexico)

Ingredients:

- 1 cup all-purpose flour
- 1 teaspoon baking powder
- 4 eggs
- 1 cup sugar
- 1 teaspoon vanilla extract
- 1 cup whole milk
- 1 can evaporated milk
- 1 can sweetened condensed milk
- 1 cup heavy cream
- 2 tablespoons sugar

Instructions:

1. Preheat oven to 350°F (175°C). Grease a 9x13-inch pan.
2. Whisk flour and baking powder together.
3. Beat eggs, sugar, and vanilla until fluffy.
4. Fold in flour mixture. Pour into pan and bake for 30 minutes.
5. Mix whole milk, evaporated milk, and condensed milk. Pour over warm cake.
6. Whip heavy cream with sugar and spread over cake. Refrigerate before serving.

Pavlova (Australia/New Zealand)

Ingredients:

- 4 egg whites
- 1 cup sugar
- 1 teaspoon vinegar
- 1 teaspoon cornstarch
- 1 teaspoon vanilla extract
- 1 cup whipped cream
- Fresh berries for topping

Instructions:

1. Preheat oven to 250°F (120°C). Line a baking sheet with parchment paper.
2. Beat egg whites until soft peaks form. Gradually add sugar, beating until glossy.
3. Fold in vinegar, cornstarch, and vanilla.
4. Shape mixture into a circle on the baking sheet.
5. Bake for 90 minutes, then let cool.
6. Top with whipped cream and berries.

Japanese Cotton Cheesecake (Japan)

Ingredients:

- 8 oz cream cheese
- 2 tablespoons butter
- ½ cup milk
- 3 eggs, separated
- ½ cup sugar
- ½ cup cake flour
- 1 teaspoon vanilla extract

Instructions:

1. Preheat oven to 325°F (160°C). Grease and line an 8-inch round pan.
2. Melt cream cheese, butter, and milk together. Let cool.
3. Beat in egg yolks, sugar, and flour.
4. In a separate bowl, beat egg whites until stiff peaks form. Fold into batter.
5. Pour batter into pan and bake in a water bath for 60 minutes.

Medovik (Russia)

Ingredients:

- ½ cup honey
- ½ cup sugar
- 2 eggs
- 2 cups flour
- 1 teaspoon baking soda
- 2 cups sour cream
- 1 cup powdered sugar

Instructions:

1. Heat honey and sugar until melted. Beat in eggs.
2. Stir in flour and baking soda. Roll into thin circles and bake at 350°F for 10 minutes.
3. Beat sour cream with powdered sugar.
4. Layer baked circles with cream. Refrigerate overnight before serving.

Cassata (Italy)

Ingredients:

- 1 sponge cake
- 2 cups ricotta cheese
- ½ cup powdered sugar
- ¼ cup chopped chocolate
- ¼ cup candied fruit
- 1 teaspoon vanilla

Instructions:

1. Cut sponge cake in layers.
2. Beat ricotta with sugar, then mix in chocolate and fruit.
3. Spread mixture between layers. Refrigerate before serving.

Chiffon Cake (United States)

Ingredients:

- 2 ¼ cups cake flour
- 1 ½ cups granulated sugar
- 1 tablespoon baking powder
- ½ teaspoon salt
- ½ cup vegetable oil
- 6 large eggs, separated
- ¾ cup water
- 1 teaspoon vanilla extract
- ½ teaspoon cream of tartar

Instructions:

1. Preheat oven to 325°F (160°C).
2. In a large bowl, whisk flour, sugar, baking powder, and salt.
3. Add egg yolks, oil, water, and vanilla. Mix until smooth.
4. In another bowl, beat egg whites with cream of tartar until stiff peaks form.
5. Gently fold egg whites into the batter.
6. Pour into an ungreased tube pan and bake for 55–60 minutes.
7. Invert pan and let cool completely before removing the cake.

Bolo de Rolo (Brazil)

Ingredients:

- 2 cups all-purpose flour
- 1 ½ cups granulated sugar
- 6 eggs
- 1 teaspoon vanilla extract
- ½ cup butter, softened
- 1 cup guava paste, melted

Instructions:

1. Preheat oven to 350°F (175°C).
2. Beat butter and sugar until fluffy. Add eggs one at a time, then mix in vanilla.
3. Gradually add flour, mixing until smooth.
4. Spread a thin layer of batter on a greased baking sheet and bake for 5–7 minutes.
5. Remove from oven, spread with melted guava paste, and roll tightly.
6. Repeat the process, layering baked sheets and rolling each time.
7. Slice and serve.

Malva Pudding (South Africa)

Ingredients:

For the Cake:

- 1 cup flour
- 1 teaspoon baking soda
- 1 cup sugar
- 1 egg
- 1 tablespoon apricot jam
- 1 tablespoon butter
- 1 teaspoon vinegar
- ½ cup milk

For the Sauce:

- 1 cup heavy cream
- ½ cup sugar
- ½ cup butter
- ½ cup hot water

Instructions:

1. Preheat oven to 350°F (175°C).
2. Mix flour and baking soda.
3. Beat egg and sugar until fluffy. Add apricot jam, butter, vinegar, and milk.
4. Fold in flour mixture and pour into a greased baking dish. Bake for 30–35 minutes.
5. For the sauce, heat cream, sugar, butter, and water until melted.
6. Pour sauce over warm cake and let soak before serving.

Dobos Torte (Hungary)

Ingredients:

- 6 large eggs
- 1 cup sugar
- 1 teaspoon vanilla extract
- 1 cup cake flour
- ½ teaspoon salt
- ½ cup unsalted butter, melted

For the Filling:

- 1 cup butter, softened
- 1 cup powdered sugar
- 8 oz melted chocolate

For the Caramel Top:

- ½ cup sugar
- 2 tablespoons water

Instructions:

1. Preheat oven to 350°F (175°C). Line six 9-inch cake pans.
2. Beat eggs and sugar until fluffy. Stir in vanilla, flour, salt, and melted butter.
3. Bake each layer for 8–10 minutes. Let cool.
4. For filling, beat butter, sugar, and melted chocolate until smooth.
5. Stack cake layers with chocolate filling in between.
6. For caramel, heat sugar and water until golden. Pour over the top layer and let set.

Kue Lapis (Indonesia)

Ingredients:

- 1 cup rice flour
- ½ cup tapioca flour
- 1 cup coconut milk
- ¾ cup sugar
- 1 teaspoon pandan extract
- Food coloring

Instructions:

1. Mix rice flour, tapioca flour, sugar, and coconut milk. Divide into two portions, one with pandan extract and green food coloring.
2. Grease a baking pan and pour a thin layer of green batter. Steam for 5 minutes.
3. Add a layer of white batter and steam again.
4. Repeat layers until batter is used up. Steam for 30 minutes.
5. Let cool, then slice into squares.

Baumkuchen (Germany)

Ingredients:

- 1 cup butter, softened
- 1 cup sugar
- 6 eggs
- 1 teaspoon vanilla extract
- 1 cup flour
- ½ teaspoon baking powder
- ¼ cup milk
- ½ teaspoon cinnamon

Instructions:

1. Preheat oven to 425°F (220°C).
2. Beat butter and sugar until creamy. Add eggs one at a time. Stir in vanilla, flour, baking powder, milk, and cinnamon.
3. Grease a cake pan and spread a thin layer of batter. Bake for 3–4 minutes.
4. Repeat with more layers, baking each until golden.
5. Let cool, then slice into layers.

Red Velvet Cake (United States)

Ingredients:

- 2 ½ cups flour
- 1 ½ cups sugar
- 1 teaspoon baking soda
- 1 teaspoon cocoa powder
- 1 cup buttermilk
- 1 cup vegetable oil
- 2 eggs
- 1 teaspoon vanilla
- 2 tablespoons red food coloring

For Frosting:

- 8 oz cream cheese
- ½ cup butter
- 2 cups powdered sugar

Instructions:

1. Preheat oven to 350°F (175°C).
2. Whisk flour, sugar, baking soda, and cocoa powder.
3. Mix buttermilk, oil, eggs, vanilla, and food coloring.
4. Combine wet and dry ingredients. Pour into cake pans and bake for 30 minutes.
5. For frosting, beat cream cheese, butter, and powdered sugar. Frost cake when cool.

Pandan Chiffon Cake (Southeast Asia)

Ingredients:

- 2 cups cake flour
- 1 ½ cups sugar
- 1 tablespoon baking powder
- ½ teaspoon salt
- 6 eggs, separated
- ¾ cup coconut milk
- ½ cup vegetable oil
- 1 teaspoon pandan extract

Instructions:

1. Preheat oven to 325°F (160°C).
2. Whisk flour, sugar, baking powder, and salt.
3. Mix egg yolks, coconut milk, oil, and pandan extract. Stir into dry ingredients.
4. Beat egg whites until stiff peaks form, then fold into batter.
5. Pour into an ungreased pan and bake for 55–60 minutes.

Mooncake (China)

Ingredients:

For Dough:

- 2 cups flour
- ¼ cup golden syrup
- 2 tablespoons vegetable oil
- ½ teaspoon baking soda

For Filling:

- 1 cup lotus seed paste
- 4 salted egg yolks

Instructions:

1. Mix flour, syrup, oil, and baking soda. Let rest for 1 hour.
2. Divide dough into small balls. Flatten and fill with lotus paste and a salted egg yolk.
3. Shape into molds.
4. Bake at 350°F (175°C) for 20 minutes.

Swedish Princess Cake (Sweden)

Ingredients:

- 1 sponge cake
- 1 cup raspberry jam
- 2 cups whipped cream
- 1 cup vanilla custard
- 1 sheet green marzipan
- Powdered sugar for dusting

Instructions:

1. Slice sponge cake into three layers.
2. Spread jam on the first layer, then custard on the second.
3. Cover with whipped cream and top with the third cake layer.
4. Roll out marzipan and cover the cake.
5. Dust with powdered sugar.

Angel Food Cake (United States)

Ingredients:

- 1 cup cake flour
- 1 ½ cups granulated sugar
- 12 large egg whites
- 1 ½ teaspoons cream of tartar
- ½ teaspoon salt
- 1 teaspoon vanilla extract

Instructions:

1. Preheat oven to 350°F (175°C).
2. Sift cake flour and ½ cup sugar together.
3. In a large bowl, beat egg whites with cream of tartar and salt until foamy.
4. Gradually add remaining sugar and beat until stiff peaks form.
5. Gently fold in flour mixture and vanilla.
6. Pour into an ungreased tube pan and bake for 35–40 minutes.
7. Invert pan and cool completely before removing.

Mille-Feuille (France)

Ingredients:

- 1 sheet puff pastry
- 1 cup pastry cream
- ½ cup powdered sugar
- ¼ cup chocolate ganache

Instructions:

1. Preheat oven to 400°F (200°C).
2. Roll out puff pastry and bake for 15–20 minutes. Let cool.
3. Cut pastry into three equal rectangles.
4. Layer pastry with pastry cream in between.
5. For topping, mix powdered sugar with a little water to make icing.
6. Spread icing on top and drizzle chocolate ganache.
7. Use a toothpick to create a marbled effect. Chill before serving.

Kransekake (Norway)

Ingredients:

- 4 cups almond flour
- 2 cups powdered sugar
- 2 egg whites

For Icing:

- 1 cup powdered sugar
- 1 egg white

Instructions:

1. Preheat oven to 375°F (190°C).
2. Mix almond flour and powdered sugar. Add egg whites and knead into a dough.
3. Roll into long ropes and shape into rings. Stack from largest to smallest.
4. Bake for 8–10 minutes until golden.
5. Mix icing ingredients and drizzle over cooled rings.

Revani (Turkey)

Ingredients:

For Cake:

- 1 cup semolina
- 1 cup flour
- ½ cup sugar
- 3 eggs
- 1 cup yogurt
- ½ cup vegetable oil
- 1 teaspoon baking powder
- Zest of 1 lemon

For Syrup:

- 2 cups sugar
- 2 cups water
- Juice of ½ lemon

Instructions:

1. Preheat oven to 350°F (175°C).
2. Beat eggs and sugar until fluffy. Add yogurt, oil, semolina, flour, baking powder, and lemon zest.
3. Pour into a greased baking pan and bake for 30 minutes.
4. Boil sugar, water, and lemon juice for 10 minutes to make syrup.
5. Pour hot syrup over warm cake. Let soak before serving.

Lamington (Australia)

Ingredients:

- 1 sponge cake, cut into squares
- 2 cups powdered sugar
- ½ cup cocoa powder
- ½ cup hot water
- 2 cups shredded coconut

Instructions:

1. Mix powdered sugar, cocoa powder, and hot water to make a glaze.
2. Dip sponge cake squares into the glaze.
3. Roll in shredded coconut.
4. Let set before serving.

Kladdkaka (Sweden)

Ingredients:

- 1 cup sugar
- ½ cup butter, melted
- 2 eggs
- ¾ cup flour
- ¼ cup cocoa powder
- 1 teaspoon vanilla extract

Instructions:

1. Preheat oven to 350°F (175°C).
2. Mix sugar and melted butter. Stir in eggs one at a time.
3. Add flour, cocoa powder, and vanilla. Mix until smooth.
4. Pour into a greased cake pan and bake for 18–20 minutes.
5. Center should be gooey. Let cool before serving.

Castella Cake (Japan)

Ingredients:

- 6 eggs
- 1 cup sugar
- 1 ½ cups bread flour
- ½ cup honey
- ¼ cup warm milk

Instructions:

1. Preheat oven to 325°F (160°C).
2. Beat eggs and sugar until pale and thick.
3. Mix honey with warm milk and fold into batter.
4. Gradually add flour, stirring gently.
5. Pour into a lined loaf pan and bake for 50 minutes.
6. Let cool before slicing.

Fruitcake (United Kingdom)

Ingredients:

- 1 cup mixed dried fruit
- ½ cup nuts, chopped
- 1 ½ cups flour
- 1 teaspoon baking powder
- ½ cup butter
- ¾ cup sugar
- 2 eggs
- ½ cup milk

Instructions:

1. Preheat oven to 325°F (160°C).
2. Cream butter and sugar. Add eggs and mix well.
3. Stir in flour, baking powder, dried fruit, and nuts.
4. Add milk and mix until combined.
5. Pour into a greased loaf pan and bake for 60 minutes.
6. Cool completely before slicing.

Bienenstich (Germany)

Ingredients:

For Cake:

- 2 cups flour
- ½ cup sugar
- ½ cup milk
- 1 packet yeast
- 2 eggs
- ¼ cup butter

For Topping:

- ½ cup butter
- ½ cup sugar
- ¼ cup honey
- ½ cup sliced almonds

Instructions:

1. Preheat oven to 350°F (175°C).
2. Mix flour, sugar, yeast, and milk. Add eggs and butter, kneading into a dough. Let rise for 1 hour.
3. Roll out dough into a baking pan.
4. Melt butter, sugar, and honey for topping. Stir in almonds.
5. Spread topping over dough and bake for 30 minutes.
6. Let cool before slicing.

Pastel de Nata (Portugal)

Ingredients:

- 1 sheet puff pastry
- 1 cup heavy cream
- ½ cup sugar
- 4 egg yolks
- 1 teaspoon vanilla extract
- ½ teaspoon cinnamon

Instructions:

1. Preheat oven to 400°F (200°C).
2. Roll out puff pastry and cut into circles. Press into muffin tins.
3. Heat cream and sugar until dissolved.
4. Whisk egg yolks with vanilla and cinnamon. Gradually mix in cream.
5. Pour into pastry shells and bake for 15–20 minutes.
6. Let cool before serving.

Esterházy Torte (Hungary)

Ingredients:

For Cake Layers:

- 6 egg whites
- 1 cup powdered sugar
- 1 ½ cups ground walnuts
- ¼ cup flour

For Cream Filling:

- 6 egg yolks
- ½ cup sugar
- 1 ½ cups milk
- 2 tablespoons cornstarch
- 1 cup butter
- 1 teaspoon vanilla extract

For Decoration:

- ½ cup apricot jam
- 1 cup white icing
- ¼ cup melted dark chocolate

Instructions:

1. Preheat oven to 320°F (160°C).
2. Beat egg whites and sugar until stiff peaks form. Fold in walnuts and flour.
3. Divide batter into 5 thin layers and bake each for 10–12 minutes. Let cool.
4. For cream, heat milk and sugar. Whisk yolks and cornstarch, then combine with milk.
5. Cook until thickened, then cool and mix in butter and vanilla.
6. Assemble by spreading cream between each layer. Cover with jam.
7. Pour white icing over top and drizzle melted chocolate. Use a toothpick to create a web pattern.

Medovnik (Czech Republic)

Ingredients:

For Cake Layers:

- ½ cup honey
- ¾ cup sugar
- 1 teaspoon baking soda
- 2 eggs
- 3 cups flour

For Filling:

- 2 cups sour cream
- 1 cup condensed milk
- ½ cup butter

Instructions:

1. Heat honey and sugar until dissolved. Add baking soda and eggs.
2. Stir in flour to form a dough, then divide into thin layers.
3. Bake each layer at 350°F (175°C) for 5 minutes.
4. Mix sour cream, condensed milk, and butter for filling.
5. Stack layers with filling in between. Let sit overnight for best flavor.

Funfetti Cake (United States)

Ingredients:

- 2 ½ cups flour
- 1 cup sugar
- ½ cup butter
- 3 eggs
- 1 cup milk
- 1 teaspoon vanilla extract
- 1 tablespoon baking powder
- ½ cup rainbow sprinkles

Instructions:

1. Preheat oven to 350°F (175°C).
2. Beat butter and sugar until fluffy. Add eggs, milk, and vanilla.
3. Mix in flour and baking powder. Fold in sprinkles.
4. Pour into greased cake pans and bake for 30 minutes.
5. Let cool before frosting with vanilla buttercream.

Hummingbird Cake (Jamaica)

Ingredients:

- 3 cups flour
- 1 cup sugar
- ½ cup brown sugar
- 1 teaspoon cinnamon
- 1 teaspoon baking soda
- 1 cup vegetable oil
- 3 eggs
- 1 cup mashed bananas
- 1 cup crushed pineapple
- ½ cup chopped pecans

Instructions:

1. Preheat oven to 350°F (175°C).
2. Mix dry ingredients. Add oil, eggs, banana, and pineapple. Stir well.
3. Fold in pecans and pour into cake pans.
4. Bake for 30–35 minutes. Cool and frost with cream cheese frosting.

Rum Cake (Caribbean)

Ingredients:

- 1 cup butter
- 2 cups sugar
- 4 eggs
- 3 cups flour
- 1 teaspoon baking powder
- ½ teaspoon salt
- 1 cup milk
- ½ cup dark rum

Instructions:

1. Preheat oven to 350°F (175°C).
2. Beat butter and sugar until fluffy. Add eggs one at a time.
3. Mix in dry ingredients alternately with milk. Stir in rum.
4. Pour into a bundt pan and bake for 45 minutes.
5. Brush extra rum over the cake while warm.

Coffee Walnut Cake (United Kingdom)

Ingredients:

- 2 cups flour
- 1 cup sugar
- ½ cup butter
- 3 eggs
- 1 teaspoon baking powder
- ¼ cup strong coffee
- ½ cup chopped walnuts

Instructions:

1. Preheat oven to 350°F (175°C).
2. Cream butter and sugar. Add eggs, coffee, and dry ingredients.
3. Fold in walnuts and pour into cake pans.
4. Bake for 25 minutes. Cool and frost with coffee buttercream.

Zebra Cake (Russia)

Ingredients:

- 2 cups flour
- 1 cup sugar
- ½ cup butter
- 3 eggs
- 1 cup milk
- 1 teaspoon vanilla
- 2 tablespoons cocoa powder

Instructions:

1. Preheat oven to 350°F (175°C).
2. Beat butter and sugar, then add eggs, milk, and vanilla.
3. Mix in flour and baking powder.
4. Divide batter in half and mix cocoa into one portion.
5. Alternate scoops of vanilla and chocolate batter in a pan.
6. Swirl slightly and bake for 40 minutes.

Honey Cake (Armenia)

Ingredients:

- ½ cup honey
- 1 cup sugar
- 3 eggs
- 2 ½ cups flour
- 1 teaspoon baking soda

For Filling:

- 2 cups sour cream
- 1 cup condensed milk

Instructions:

1. Heat honey and sugar. Add eggs and baking soda. Stir in flour.
2. Roll into thin layers and bake at 350°F (175°C) for 5 minutes each.
3. Mix sour cream and condensed milk for filling.
4. Assemble layers with filling in between. Let sit overnight.

King Cake (France/Louisiana)

Ingredients:

- 4 cups flour
- ½ cup sugar
- 2 teaspoons yeast
- ½ cup warm milk
- 2 eggs
- ½ cup butter

For Filling:

- ½ cup brown sugar
- 2 teaspoons cinnamon
- ½ cup pecans

For Glaze:

- 1 cup powdered sugar
- 2 tablespoons milk

Instructions:

1. Dissolve yeast in warm milk. Add flour, sugar, eggs, and butter. Knead and let rise.
2. Roll out dough and spread filling. Roll into a ring shape.
3. Bake at 375°F (190°C) for 25 minutes.
4. Glaze with icing and decorate with colored sugar.

Mawa Cake (India)

Ingredients:

- 1 cup mawa (khoya)
- ½ cup sugar
- ½ cup butter
- 2 eggs
- 1 ½ cups flour
- ½ teaspoon cardamom
- ½ cup milk

Instructions:

1. Preheat oven to 350°F (175°C).
2. Cream butter, sugar, and mawa. Add eggs.
3. Mix in flour, cardamom, and milk.
4. Pour into a pan and bake for 30 minutes.

Napoleon Cake (Russia)

Ingredients:

For Pastry Layers:

- 3 ½ cups flour
- 1 cup cold butter
- 1 egg
- ½ cup cold water
- 1 teaspoon vinegar
- 1 pinch salt

For Cream Filling:

- 3 cups milk
- ¾ cup sugar
- 3 egg yolks
- 3 tablespoons cornstarch
- 1 teaspoon vanilla

Instructions:

1. Cut butter into flour until crumbly. Mix in egg, water, vinegar, and salt.
2. Knead dough, divide into 8 parts, and chill for 1 hour.
3. Roll out each piece into a thin sheet and bake at 375°F (190°C) for 7 minutes.
4. For cream, heat milk and sugar. Whisk yolks and cornstarch, then combine with milk.
5. Cook until thick, then cool.
6. Assemble layers with cream. Let sit overnight before serving.

Pão de Ló (Portugal)

Ingredients:

- 6 eggs
- 1 cup sugar
- 1 cup flour
- 1 teaspoon baking powder
- 1 teaspoon vanilla

Instructions:

1. Preheat oven to 350°F (175°C).
2. Beat eggs and sugar until fluffy.
3. Fold in flour, baking powder, and vanilla.
4. Pour into a greased pan and bake for 25 minutes.

Punschkrapfen (Austria)

Ingredients:

For Cake:

- 4 eggs
- 1 cup sugar
- 1 cup flour
- ½ teaspoon baking powder

For Filling:

- ½ cup apricot jam
- ¼ cup rum
- 1 cup chopped sponge cake (leftover)

For Glaze:

- 2 cups powdered sugar
- 2 tablespoons rum
- Red food coloring

Instructions:

1. Bake sponge cake at 350°F (175°C) for 25 minutes. Let cool.
2. Cut cake into squares and mix leftover cake crumbs with jam and rum.
3. Sandwich filling between cake squares.
4. Mix glaze ingredients, tint pink, and coat cakes.

Orange Olive Oil Cake (Spain)

Ingredients:

- 2 cups flour
- 1 cup sugar
- ½ cup olive oil
- 3 eggs
- ½ cup orange juice
- 1 teaspoon baking powder
- Zest of 1 orange

Instructions:

1. Preheat oven to 350°F (175°C).
2. Beat eggs and sugar. Add olive oil and orange juice.
3. Mix in flour, baking powder, and zest.
4. Pour into a pan and bake for 35 minutes.

Banana Cake (Philippines)

Ingredients:

- 2 cups flour
- 1 teaspoon baking soda
- ½ teaspoon salt
- 1 cup sugar
- ½ cup butter
- 2 eggs
- 1 cup mashed bananas
- ½ cup milk

Instructions:

1. Preheat oven to 350°F (175°C).
2. Beat butter and sugar, then add eggs.
3. Mix in dry ingredients, followed by bananas and milk.
4. Pour into a pan and bake for 40 minutes.

Sans Rival (Philippines)

Ingredients:

For Meringue Layers:

- 6 egg whites
- ¾ cup sugar
- 1 teaspoon vanilla
- 1 cup chopped cashews

For Buttercream:

- 6 egg yolks
- ¾ cup sugar
- 1 cup butter
- 2 tablespoons water

Instructions:

1. Beat egg whites and sugar to stiff peaks. Fold in vanilla and cashews.
2. Bake in thin layers at 300°F (150°C) for 20 minutes.
3. For buttercream, cook yolks, sugar, and water until thick.
4. Mix in butter and cool.
5. Assemble layers with buttercream.

Buko Pandan Cake (Philippines)

Ingredients:

For Cake:

- 2 cups flour
- 1 cup sugar
- ½ cup butter
- 3 eggs
- 1 teaspoon pandan extract
- 1 teaspoon baking powder

For Frosting:

- 1 cup whipped cream
- ½ cup shredded coconut (buko)

Instructions:

1. Preheat oven to 350°F (175°C).
2. Cream butter and sugar, then add eggs and pandan.
3. Mix in dry ingredients.
4. Pour into a pan and bake for 35 minutes.
5. Frost with whipped cream and top with coconut.

Chocolate Biscuit Cake (Ireland)

Ingredients:

- 2 cups crushed digestive biscuits
- ½ cup butter
- ½ cup sugar
- ½ cup cocoa powder
- ½ cup milk
- 1 cup melted chocolate

Instructions:

1. Melt butter and sugar. Stir in cocoa and milk.
2. Mix with crushed biscuits.
3. Press into a pan and refrigerate for 2 hours.
4. Pour melted chocolate over the top and let set.

Dulce de Leche Cake (Argentina)

Ingredients:

For Cake:

- 3 cups flour
- 1 teaspoon baking powder
- 1 cup sugar
- ½ cup butter
- 3 eggs
- 1 cup milk

For Filling & Topping:

- 1 ½ cups dulce de leche

Instructions:

1. Preheat oven to 350°F (175°C).
2. Cream butter and sugar, then add eggs.
3. Mix in dry ingredients and milk.
4. Bake for 30 minutes.
5. Spread dulce de leche between layers and on top.

Ma Lai Gao (China)

Ingredients:

- 2 cups cake flour
- 1 cup sugar
- 3 eggs
- 1 cup evaporated milk
- 1 teaspoon baking powder
- 1 teaspoon vanilla

Instructions:

1. Beat eggs and sugar until fluffy.
2. Fold in milk, flour, and baking powder.
3. Steam in a bamboo steamer for 40 minutes.